Ladybugs

To my dad

Ladybugs

Red,
Fiery,
and
Bright

by
Mia Posada

194 Clearview place
Felton ca.

SCHOLASTIC INC.

New York Toronto London Auckland Sydney
Mexico City New Delhi Hong Kong Buenos Aires

Little round beetles
with red coats and black spots

crawl through gardens and trees,
and on flowers in pots.

They are ladybugs!

A crawling ladybug
tickles your arm.
But this little insect will
cause you no harm.

They are busy
searching for food to eat.
Tiny green insects
called aphids taste sweet.

A ladybug may flee in fear from a
hungry bird landing near.

But eating a ladybug is a waste—
to birds, they have a terrible taste!

When a female ladybug
has eggs to be laid,
she finds a safe place
on a leaf in the shade.

In five days,
the yellow eggs
will turn white.

The hatching day
is now within sight.

Tiny creatures climb out
from the creamy white eggs.
They have hairy gray bodies
and long skinny legs.

They are called **larvae**.

Hungry larvae search
for food right away.
They can eat
one hundred aphids
a day!

A larva's skin cannot stretch,
and since this is so,
it must shed its old skin in order
to grow.

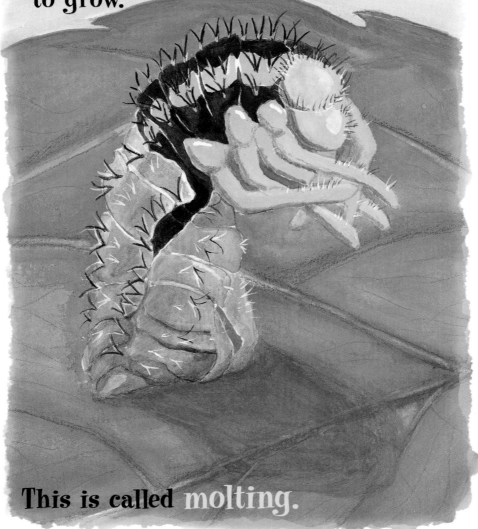

This is called molting.

Its skin splits apart.
The larva wiggles free.

Its new larger skin
fits more comfortably.

When a ladybug larva
is almost full grown,
it attaches itself to a plant or a
stone.

It molts
one last time
the skin
it outgrew.

When it
emerges,
it has become
something new. It is a *pupa*.

The pupa is covered by a tough orange skin.
It hides the changes taking place within.

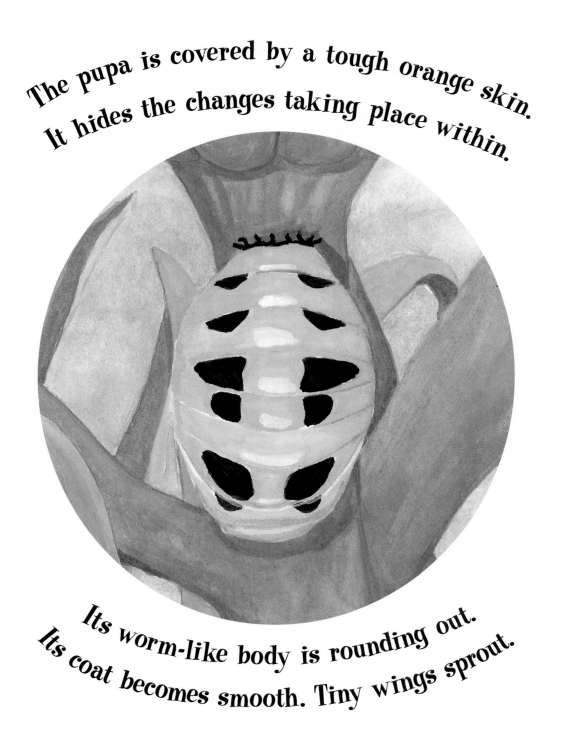

Its worm-like body is rounding out.
Its coat becomes smooth. Tiny wings sprout.

In five days,
the pupa's shell starts to crack.

A beetle crawls out
with no spots on its back.

Soon black spots come into sight.
The yellow coat turns to red,
fiery and bright.

The new ladybug
spreads its wings out to dry.

A few hours pass, then it's able to fly.

Its spotted wing-covers move off to the sides.

It beats its wings,

and away it glides.

The new ladybugs with
red coats and black spots

crawl through gardens and trees,
and on flowers in pots.

More about Ladybugs

There are many different kinds of ladybugs. Some are red, orange, or yellow with black spots or patterns. Others are black with red or yellow marks. Shown here are a few of the many types of ladybugs.

eyed ladybug
Anatis Ocellata

Ladybugs are members of the large group of insects called beetles. The scientific name for the ladybug family is Coccinellidae (cock-si-NEL-li-dee). There are about four thousand different species, or kinds, of ladybugs throughout the world. They range in size from about 0.08 to 0.5 inch (2 to 12 mm). Ladybugs are also called ladybird beetles. Their name dates back hundreds of years to the Middle Ages. The beetle was dedicated to Mary, the mother of Jesus, who was called "Our Lady." Regardless of their name, there are both male and female ladybugs.

ten-spotted ladybug
Adalia 10-punctata

Rodalia cardinalis

Ladybugs are active in the spring and summer, and their lifespan is about three weeks. At the end of the summer when cold weather begins, ladybugs hibernate, or rest quietly, in large groups. They may hibernate in safe places such as inside hollow logs or under rocks. When the temperature warms up to about 60ºF (15ºC), the ladybugs become active again.

two-spotted ladybug
Adalia bipunctat

Ladybugs are not fast fliers, but they use other methods to keep away from predators, or animals that want to eat them. When disturbed, ladybugs ooze a bitter orange liquid from the joints of their legs. This liquid tastes unpleasant to predators, and they soon learn to leave the spotted insects alone. Ladybugs also protect themselves by lying on their backs and folding up their legs, or "playing dead."

ash-gray ladybug
Olla sayi

seven-spotted ladybug
Coccinella 7-punctata

Ladybugs are perhaps the most popular of all beetles because they are very helpful to people. They eat huge numbers of small insects called aphids. Aphids suck the juices from plants such as roses and wheat. They may destroy a farmer's whole crop or a whole garden of flowers. For many centuries, farmers have depended on ladybugs to protect their crops from aphids. Ladybugs also eat other insect pests, called mites, and scale insects that destroy orange, apple, and other fruit trees. People breed, or raise, ladybugs and sell large clusters of them to farmers who set them free in their fields. The ladybugs go to work eating insect pests so the plants can grow. Perhaps this is why ladybugs have long been thought to bring good luck.

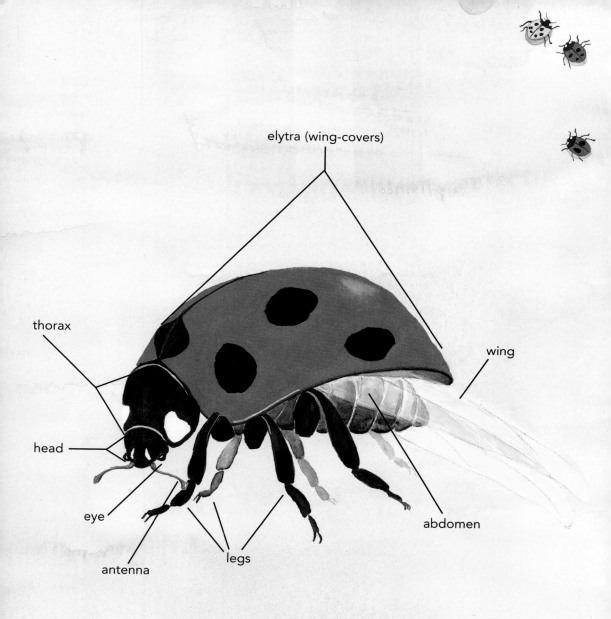

elytra (wing-covers)

thorax

head

eye

antenna

legs

wing

abdomen

ISBN 0-439-66472-1

12 11 10 9 8 7 6 5   4 5 6 7 8 9/0

Printed in the U.S.A.   23

First Scholastic printing, May 2004